In *this first mini-book of a series, psychologist Nathan Ory points out that children with "special needs" can sometimes express normal behavior, a fact that misleads some adults into concluding that the child just needs to "try harder", and that the parents are just "spoiling" the child. The author compassionately and articulately unveils this common pattern and gives the parent permission and specific tips for supporting and protecting the child from the expectations of the uninformed others. Moreover, he gives numerous examples and helpful tips for recognizing and managing the many "invisible" challenges of children, such as problems with attention, distractibility, processing speed, and memory that are ubiquitous among children today. As such, this book will be useful to a wide audience of parents and professionals that interact with children. It offers a fresh, diagnostic-free, individualized approach to helping children that is insightful and extremely practical. A must read!*

Donald T. Saposnek, Ph.D.
Clinical-Child Psychologist
Department of Psychology
University of California, Santa Cruz

WHEN YOU SEE CONFUSION,
OFFER A PEACEFUL, HELPING HAND.

**PRACTICAL APPROACHES TO CHALLENGING
BEHAVIORS IN PEOPLE WITH SPECIAL NEEDS**

SURVIVAL TIPS FROM PSYCHOLOGIST
NATHAN ORY
(WITH STUDY GUIDES)

BOOK ONE

HOW DO I EXPLAIN TO OTHERS WHAT IS HAPPENING WITH MY CHILD?

Nathan E. Ory, M.A.
Registered Psychologist
Challenging Behavior Analysis and Consultation, Ltd.
543 Marine View,
Cobble Hill,
British Columbia, V0R 1L1
challengingbehavior@shaw.ca
Phone: (250) 743-1667

OCT – – 2014

Original cover art by Bonnie A. Ory.

Typeset in Plantin with Trade Gothic display
at SpicaBookDesign

Printed and bound with www.createspace.com

CA(71)

TABLE OF CONTENTS

INTRODUCTION TO THIS SERIES

As a registered psychologist, for 40 years I have been training parents, teachers, support workers, social workers and mental health professionals. Following my work doing functional behavior analysis of hundreds of cases I have been teaching others about how to find the "windows of opportunity" that may open the door to positive relationship with individuals with challenging behaviors and a wide variety of developmental disabilities.

The children, youth and adults I have seen who have a specific diagnosis have usually had more than one diagnosis. Many have had no specific diagnosis but have displayed similar functional and behavioral issues. In this series I do not specify the diagnosis of the individuals described. The functional behaviors outlined here may be seen in many diagnosed conditions. The presence or absence of the functional behaviors I describe do not confirm or deny any one particular diagnosis.

Nathan's Note:

Who will this book help? Those on the autism and fetal alcohol spectrum. People with intellectual disabilities, learning disabilities and other brain dysfunctions.

The functional deficits that lead to challenging behaviors observed in those with autism spectrum disorder, fetal alcohol spectrum disorder, intellectual disabilities and that are in common with some learning disabilities may also be observed in persons with other brain dysfunctions such as acquired brain injury through trauma, illness or stroke, psychiatric disorders and dementia. The practical suggestions for support of the functional deficits described in this series may be useful for any of these conditions.

Many of the participants in my trainings have requested something they could have on hand to explain to others in a simple manner some of the extremely complex issues with the persons they were supporting. This is the purpose of this "mini-book" series that I am creating to accompany the 2007 edition of my book, "Working with People with Challenging Behavior."

I am able to write this series because, from the beginning of my career, when I would first attempt to explain the results of my assessments to my wife Bonnie in her role as a special educator she would ask me, "what exactly does that mean?" I re-wrote until I was able to make explicit the practical implications of what test results meant to the assessed individual and to the people trying to give them the support they required.

For her infinite patience and for her invaluable editing I dedicate this series to my wife, Bonnie Ory, who has always believed that "some day you will write about all of this."

"How do I explain to others what is happening with my child?"

"No one believes me."

In the story below, Jen and her son Michael are an unfortunate yet typical example of what often occurs when a child has a subtle learning disability where the child sometimes appears "perfectly normal" and at other times is completely unable to cope without special accommodation. Similar issues arise with parents of children and adults who have intellectual disabilities, fetal alcohol spectrum disorder, autism spectrum disorder and other brain dysfunctions but sometimes display "perfectly normal" behavior.

It is difficult to tell just one "story" that is relevant to every reader. When I speak of individuals who are non-verbal I am asked, how is that relevant to those who are verbal? And vice-versa. When I speak of those who are "high-functioning" I am asked, how is that relevant to those who are "low functioning?" And vice-versa. The "typical" story below is used to introduce you, the reader to the emotional space that is shared by the support persons of all of these individuals. In the sections on approaches to challenging behavior I relate

> Quotable quote:
>
> "Others are looking constantly over my shoulder and second-guessing everything I do."

examples that are relevant to all of the above. While the following begins with a story about a mother of a child with a subtle learning disability the situation may apply equally to those supporting an individual with any developmental disability.

Jen and mothers like her are often criticized by others who do not have the same first-hand experience of understanding what is going on with their children. Jen and mothers like her receive the non-verbal, raised eyebrow or deep sigh from others. They receive direct verbal criticism and sarcastic remarks from others who just don't believe it is possible for someone who can do so well "some of the time" may be unable to **always** do as well.

The purpose of this small book is to offer parents such as Jen something that they can hand to those who they feel are "looking constantly over my shoulder and second-guessing everything I do."

A typical story:

Michael's mother Jen sits at the kitchen table, her left hand on her forehead, her head suddenly too heavy to hold up by itself. Her right hand lay slightly shaking, while holding onto her half empty, cooling cup of coffee. Jen's shoulders are heaving, tears running down her face, dropping slowly onto the document lying on the table in front of her. This was Michael's third suspension notice so far this school year, and it wasn't even February.

Jen understands that other parents are putting a lot of pressure on the school. Some parents have requested that their children be moved from Michael's class. At great cost, two parents have already moved their children to a local private school. One parent is threatening to sue the school district to recover the cost of private school, saying that the only reason they had to do this was because the school told them they were unable to move their own child to another classroom.

But, it was all so unnecessary. This is what defeated Jen. Jen had explained to the teacher so many times that Michael can't be rushed. Nobody seems to believe how devastating it is to Michael when he feels that he has to rush to keep up with the others. When he sees others finishing before he is finished he becomes extremely anxious. If they would just give him more time in an area where he can't observe what the others are doing he can be fine. Michael is such a perfectionist he can't stand not working as quickly as the other children in his class.

Jen has explained that Michael always gives plenty of signals that he is going to melt down. The issue is that sometimes Michael can work just as quickly as the others without any problem. Michael is usually OK when he has lots of sleep the night before, isn't hungry and has had plenty of exercise the day before. It seems to take all of Michael's energy for "all the points in his mind to line up" so that he can focus without being excessively distracted.

When Michael is tired, hungry or low energy he almost always becomes fidgety. Jen has explained that they should be on the lookout for times when Michael's eyes become "squinty" and his vision seems to be darting around the room. Jen has told the teachers that when Michael is particularly anxious they would know this because he will hold his breath and his handwriting is shakier than normal for him. These are the signs that Michael needs to be coached to stop concentrating on whatever is being expected of him at the moment.

Why does no one take her seriously when she explains this to them? All they need to do when they see this happening with Michael is to go up to him and give him some other small, meaningful job to do. All they need to do is to offer him a way out of the situation he is in at that moment so he can stop comparing his own work to that of the students around him.

Nathan's note:

Michael is trying too hard to be "normal" at a time when he just can't get his brain to do it.

When Michael is fidgeting and his eyes are darting and he is holding his breath, to ask Michael to continue his efforts with a comment such as "just a few more" is like rubbing his nose in his sense of being "different" from the other students. This is what causes him to melt down. *Michael is trying too hard to be "normal" at a time when he just can't get his brain to do it.*

Jen knows that many people just can not wrap their minds around how it is possible for Michael to do perfectly well some of the time under what is for Michael, "normal" circumstances; and at other times Michael acts like an agitated, angry, reactive, oppositional, manipulative and spoiled child who will only do things "his own way."

Not too many people seem to believe Jen when she explains how sad Michael is when he comes home after a melt-down where he has gotten into trouble and the principal had to be called into the room. Michael blames himself and is so ashamed of him self. Michael cries to his mother, "I should never have been born." And, "I'm just so stupid." It breaks Jen's heart. Jen is usually able to cheer Michael up by talking with him about his wonderful drawings and getting him to dance with her. Michael is a really good dancer and sometimes feels better when Jen asks him to teach her a new dance step.

Study guide

Think about how Michael's story relates to someone that you are supporting.

a.) Michael tends to melt down if he is rushed or if he observes others finishing before he is finished. What are the two or three similar things that you recognize will tend to cause the person you are supporting to melt down?

b.) Michael is sometimes able to tolerate being rushed or not finishing at the same time of others. But Michael has no tolerance or resilience if he is hungry, over-tired, or if he has not had enough exercise. Have you recognized any similar sort of conditions applying to the person you are supporting? List them.

c.) Michael always gives signals that he is getting ready to melt down. "Squinty eyes", darting eyes, holding his breath, shaky handwriting. As soon as this is observed Michael needs to be offered a way out of the situation, perhaps with a small meaningful job such as to empty the wastebasket. Have you observed any similar sort of early warning signals with the person you are supporting? List them here.

d.) Have you found that giving some distracting, helpful job helps to calm down the person you are supporting? What are some of these?

e.) When he calls himself "stupid" Jen tries to cheer up Michael by talking to him about a drawing of his or by asking him to teach her a new dance step. Think about the types of things you do or might be able to do to change the mood of the person you are supporting when they display self-rejection. What strengths do they have that you can focus on with them? List these.

Jen feels distressed about how to explain Michael to others so that they will understand and believe what Michael is going through. How to get others to accept that Michael is able to both be "normal" and also outrageously "abnormal" in his behavior? How to get others to understand and accommodate to Michael's "special needs" even though he does not qualify for any sort of individual education or individual program plan? Almost everyone simply "judges" Michael as lacking self-control and as "doing his behavior." What Jen hears most often is, "If Michael can do quite well some of the time, that means his behavior is under his own self-control and he has to learn to be self-controlled all of the time."

It wasn't always as bad as it became this year when Michael went into grade five. When Michael was in grade three he had one teacher, Ms. Cabral who seemed to understand how things worked for Michael. She really seemed to appreciate Michael's fine sense of humour and to recognize how hard he was trying. When Michael started to show any signs of agitation Ms. Cabral seemed to have a sixth sense about when he needed her to be closer to him to help him calm down and focus on just one small thing that he could do at a time; or she would distract him into some other, helpful role.

At the recent school meeting Jen was told that Michael's problems were not "bad enough" to get him the extra attention that he only needed at certain times. But why, Jen had demanded could they not see that at those certain times it was <u>critical</u> for Michael to have the extra attention to help him calm down and stay focused on what he <u>could</u> do well?

Jen and Michael both missed Ms. Cabral and the smaller classroom of the earlier grade. Sometimes

Michael would ask, "Why can't I have Ms. Cabral as my teacher? She never made me mad." When he was in grade three the main emphasis wasn't on the curriculum. But, now in grade five it was all about "getting the work done on time" and the teacher had three other children with designated learning disabilities in her classroom that demanded all of her "extra" time.

It is even hard for Jen to get her own family to see that Michael is not just "doing his behavior." Jen's husband, Jack sometimes seems to accept that how Michael behaves depends on how well Michael is <u>able</u> at the moment to control his level of internal agitation and to self-calm. But even though Jack seems to accept this, Jack still sometimes loses his temper at Michael when he is in a melt-down, and this always makes things escalate even further. For Jen, at these times it is like she has two children that she has to calm down. This makes Jen feel even more alone with the burden of loving and understanding her son, and trying to protect him from circumstances where she knows things are going to be just too much for him to handle.

Jen also is burdened by the "flack" she sometimes is exposed to from her sister-in-law as well as from her own mother who tell her that she is "coddling" Michael too much when he acts out. He never acts out with them. (Of

Nathan's note:

It is hard for Jen to not feel guilty and doubt herself and her own judgement.

course not, Jen thinks. They never have to make any demands of Michael to get out the door on time.) On top of that insult they also say to her, "Michael has to learn that there isn't always going to be someone to protect him." And "How is he ever going to learn to manage his own behavior better if Jen keeps protecting him from the consequences of his actions by standing up for him all the time?" Parents and special educators frequently hear these same complaints.

Jen's sister-in-law and mother openly criticise Jen for giving Michael the sense that it "isn't his fault" when he loses it. When Jack is silent while this criticism is being dished out Jen feels that Jack is sabotaging her. It is hard for Jen to not feel guilty and doubt herself and her own judgement. If Jen can't even make her own family understand what she knows is the truth about Michael how is she ever going to get Michael the protection and special assistance he requires before he is completely abandoned by the school system?

Study guide

Does this sound like a familiar story to you?

a.) Who are the people in your own support system that you can honestly talk to about how alone you may be feeling in your knowledge that there is a "right way" or at least a "best way" to do things with the child you are supporting?

b.) If you don't have anyone you can talk to, are you aware of your local associations for support to parents of children with learning disabilities or developmental disabilities? Have you tried to ask for a personal meeting with the school counselor or someone in the school administration responsible for special education?

Personal note from Nathan to my reader

It isn't just parents who have this difficulty explaining their child to his teachers or other family members. It is natural for anyone's first response to extreme behavior to be primarily concerned about the effect of the disruptive behaviors on the classroom and other children. Only after things have calmed down is there time to think about what else might be going on with the child underneath their behavior.

Teachers have asked me, "How do I get the other teachers (or teaching assistants) to understand?" Classroom and community support workers who have an intuitive sense that "something else is going on here" have expressed to me the same difficulty getting other support workers with the same child to accept the need for an alternative, more supportive approach.

Mental health counselors have also asked me, "How do I get the parent to understand that there are other ways to approach their child without provoking a reaction?"

If you have read this far I want to thank you for caring about mothers like Jen and the children like Michael that you may have come across in your own lives. If you are a mother like Jen or a child like Michael I want to thank you for surviving the criticisms of others who don't seem to "get" what your life experiences have been like.

If the "Michael" you know has had psychological assessments you will likely have been told that there is a wide range of strengths and weaknesses in the test results. Issues will likely have been in one or more of the following areas: speed of processing; attention and distractibility; short term memory; dealing with complexity; dealing with abstract; problems in organization and planning; and impulsivity.

For the "Michael" you know who has had occupational therapy assessments, among other things you will likely have been told that there are issues with sensory seeking and/or sensory avoidance; difficulty with planning and coordinating movements; and problems with under and/or over arousal and impulsivity.

For the "Michael" you know who has had speech language assessments you will likely have been told that there are issues in understanding time concepts, use of pragmatic language, and many other subtle, individual issues that the speech therapist will have described.

For the "Michael" you know who has had behavioral assessment you will likely have been told that there are issues with need to control; resistive and oppositional behavior; inability to delay gratification; anxiety when uncertain; frustration with failure; inability to tolerate correction or criticism; explosive reaction to rejection; high sensitivity/reactivity to tone of voice and physical posture of support persons.

In the behavioral assessment there will likely be comments about areas where there is a strong desire to please; ability to work well with those who are calm and consistent; ability to do his best in a highly predictable and structured environment; need for frequent and specific feedback about acceptable and appropriate behavior; and difficulty generalizing from one context to another. You will have heard comments such as "He will do well with familiar tasks in familiar situations and yet do poorly on the same tasks in unfamiliar situations." "He will do well with some people no matter what the task and yet do poorly with other people no matter what the task!"

My experience with the many "Michaels" I have worked with is that they are most often trying their hardest and doing the best they can with what they have got to work with. Sometimes it is an issue that expectations for the child are, at that moment, too high for the child to meet. Sometimes it is an issue that the child's own expectations for themselves are, at that moment, unachievable.

In the balance of this small book I will be describing many examples of how the issues listed above could affect the "Michael" you may be supporting; how to explain these issues to others; and what you can do that may be effective in making it easier for the "Michael" you know to be successful so that he or she can feel competent, acknowledged and accepted for who he or she is.

I have attached an article I first wrote over 15 years ago titled, "Who has to change?" This is the article that I am asked most frequently for permission to include on the web pages of organizations supporting those with subtle learning problems and challenging behavior. I have brought this article up to date and included it here for you to be able to show to others who just don't believe what you are trying to explain to them about the strengths you see in your child.

General approach to challenging behavior

Regardless of the person's diagnosis, people who have melt downs and express rage some of the time, but at other times are basically OK tend to have episodes of acting in situations where they require at that moment more support than is available. In order to be successful and not get hit or bit, in difficult moments it is a good idea to lower expectations for independent achievement. At the same time, raise expectations for relationship sustaining and peaceful participation. For a person who may suddenly act out with extreme irritability, "keeping the peace" is more important than getting work done. Base expectations on how successful the person can be while at the same time, remaining calm, focused and self-controlled.

For example: For one child the "curriculum" might be to give her something to do that she is able to do without provoking an episode of scratching herself and screaming. Try to keep her "below her threshold" for becoming highly aroused. If this means doing coloring instead of doing math, at least school will become a place of calm and safety for her and others.

For example: For one child the "curriculum" might be to peacefully complete the small amount of work at grade level that he is able to do before he becomes too anxious about being perfect, and then move back to easier work that the child can still do with enthusiasm.

Too many unnecessary conflicts occur when an attitude of "well, they have to learn to be independent" is preventing taking an approach where the person might be successful, but more dependent. Raise expectations for spontaneous cooperation at what the person is able to routinely do well. Try to give positive control to the person under guidance and structure.

For example: If the child can't read or is unwilling to read at that moment, then offer them an opportunity to hold the book, sitting quietly beside you, and to turn the page while you are reading it aloud to them. In this manner you are engaged in relationship sustaining behavior with the child who is not being asked to do anything that they could possibly fail at doing.

Study guide

a.) List one or two examples of situations that you can describe for the person you are supporting where you believe "keeping the peace" would be a more useful approach than "getting the work done." Think about examples where you gave the person something to do that you knew was "too easy" for her, but she settled right down and independently did and accepted this, more familiar work.

b.) List one or two examples of situations where you were observing resistance and agitation when the person you are supporting was asked to "do it on your own" but you found that you were able to keep the person happy and calm by asking them to "help" <u>you</u> do something that you knew they "should have" been able to do on their own.

In this small book I will be talking about the following types of "invisible disabilities" that are commonly found in those who present with challenging behavior: Slow pace of thinking; distractibility and inattention; issues with memory and complexity; time concepts and transitions.

Slow pace of thinking

Slower thinking may be the most common "invisible disability" that leads to what is often interpreted as resistive and oppositional behavior. Several examples demonstrate where the resistance and opposition is completely avoidable.

An example is the person who always says "no" as soon as you ask him to do anything, such as to take out the garbage. If you ask him a second time he might blow up at you, telling you to "stop nagging me." But if you wait twenty seconds and don't say anything else he initiates and follows the request or direction on his own. Or, if you simply pick up the garbage can and hand it to him, he takes it from you and cooperatively follows the implied direction.

Nathan's note:

Ask, does resistance mean, "I don't want to do it?" Or, does it mean, "I need more time to think about it?" What you thought was resistance could be a "counterfeit" behavior.

An example is the person who, if you ask her to clean up her room she reacts as if this is a demand that she immediately stop what she is doing. She yells at you to "Leave me alone!" But if you write down "Time to clean your room" and slip it under her bedroom door she comes out of her room ten minutes later with pride and looking for approval for having cleaned up her room all on her own.

An example is the person who is frustrated and reactive if you single him out and ask him to do something such as to get out a certain book, or put on his sports gear. But if you make the request of a group of people, he sits back until everyone else has started to do the requested activity, and then he cooperatively joins in.

An example is the person who simply doesn't "get it" when she is only asked or told to do something one time. For her, it takes more repetitions for what you say to "sink in." For some people who are unresponsive you may have to repeat your comment or give your direction again 30 seconds later and they are then immediately responsive. For some people who are unresponsive you may have to inform them five minutes ahead of time that in a few minutes you will be asking them to do something. Then ask them in five minutes and they are immediately responsive.

These examples are all indications of resistive or oppositional behaviors that are not actually behavior problems. These are examples of what I call "counterfeit behaviors." These examples are actually all indications of "I need more time to think about it problem" or "I need to <u>see</u> it happening before I can do it problem."

Experiments to see if the person is willing, but experiencing slow thinking:

- Wait 20 seconds before you make a request a second time.
- Write down your request.

- Make your request to a group.
- Repeat your request after 30 seconds.
- Tell the person now what you are going to tell them in five minutes.

What is so hard for others to understand is the person is sometimes slower thinking, yet at other times is quick to respond and doesn't require extra repetition, demonstration or handling with "kid gloves." The responses of some people are variable based on their motivation or interest at the moment; whether or not they are distracted; if they are fatigued; as well as who is doing the asking and their immediate situations. It is hard for those who see such variability to accept that just because the person can do it perfectly well some of the time, that doesn't necessarily mean that they can do it the same way all of the time; or even just a few minutes later.

In the many groups I have led almost everyone in the room knows some individuals who have these or similar, personally unique ways where it seems to work best for them if you approach them in manner that is particularly suited to their slower pace of processing information or requests. To my own astonishment as well as those in these groups, almost <u>none</u> of the recognized, idiosyncratic ways of getting the best response to requests or directions from a student were written down or communicated among support persons. Yet slower pace of thinking can account for a great deal of what is otherwise interpreted as resistive and oppositional behavior.

> THE "FOLKLORE" OF EACH PERSON IS THE ORAL, NARRATIVE HISTORY AND STORIES THAT REVEAL WHO A PERSON REALLY IS. THE "FOLKLORE" OF EACH PERSON INSTRUCTS US ABOUT THE ACCURATE BELIEFS WE SHOULD HOLD ABOUT THE PERSON.

I suggest that if there is anything that support persons have noticed about a unique, "best way" to pace instruction, information or directions, this should be written down and should become part of the "folklore" for this student. No one who is expected to interact with a person who can be highly resistive should engage with them without first knowing the fundamentals of how to assist them to hear and process what is being asked of them.

There is no way to predict how this will work for any one individual. If you suspect "slow processing" may be part of the equation behind resistive and oppositional behavior it is necessary to experiment. Your "target" for change is not the person's challenging behavior, but your relationship with and supporting the person as they are! Move forward with the individual the way they are, not as the system they are in expects them to be.

What you can do when <u>you</u> don't know for sure what to do?

- It is always helpful to give a person more time to process.
- It's always helpful to only give a person only one thing at a time.
- Wait for completion of the first thing before giving him the next thing to do.
- It's often helpful to let her watch you showing someone else first.

It is often helpful to take the approach that "nothing counts till you are ready." This removes any sense of time pressure to respond. Allow him as many "practices" as he seems to need to keep his anxiety at a minimum.

NOTE: These examples about slow pace of thinking are quite different from the person who is only able to process when he has advance warning about anything that is going to be coming up next. Those are not issues with slow processing. Those are issues with needing predictability and no surprises. I address those types of issues in a future, small book dedicated to assisting those who have difficulties with anxiety and transitions.

When you suspect slower pace of thinking is part of the problem the following are the types of questions you should be trying to answer for the person you are supporting.

Experiment and record:
    a.) How long does it typically take the person to respond to a request or direction? Do the experiment. Observe and record this.

    b.) How do you tell when the person is done one thing and ready for the next thing?

    c.) Is there a pattern in how long it takes the person to respond? All the time the same, one way? Sometimes faster or slower but only under certain circumstances?

    d.) Can you identify the circumstances where the person will most typically demonstrate slower pace of thinking? Faster pace?

    e.) What types of approaches have you found that work best? Are there any approaches that you know must never be used? These are the "Do's" and "Don't do's" for this person. These are an aspect of the child's "folklore." If the"Do's and Don't Do's" that you have discovered are not included in a behavior/ teaching plan, write these down and discuss with everyone who is involved in supporting this child.

Distractibility and inattention

The background here is that often youth with problems in short-term memory, distractibility and inattention have become used to the experience of receiving mostly negative feedback when they have <u>not</u> done as they were asked to do. People around them tend to base their expectation on "If you can do this thing some of the time, then you should be able to do that other thing just as well." Unfortunately, sometimes this is just not the case.

One young woman was able to do familiar school work at the grade seven level. Her problem solving and comprehension was at the grade-three level. She was quite good at helping out with janitorial work in a local church. When she was working alone in the church she could independently follow up to four directions in a sequence. However, if there was even one other person anywhere in the church while she was working she was unable to concentrate and complete even one of her familiar tasks. She was just too distractible.

It is difficult to understand and accept the extreme variability that is shown by people who can be independently competent, some of the time, and in particular circumstances; yet quite disorganized, incompetent and dependent at other times. Below I will describe some of the influences that can affect the variability of a person's ability to attend and sustain their focus.

Example: Motivation can affect ability to focus.

One student is able to concentrate well when he is over-focused and doing something that is of extreme interest to him. He is able to repair bicycle gears and brakes. It turns out that the only way he can focus is when he is motivated and over-focused. When he is not focused on something of strong personal interest his attention seems to "hop, skip and jump" all around, and he impulsively engages with whatever is happening around him.

Teaching tip for distractibility due to lack of motivation

Notice if the person you are supporting is able to attend and concentrate well and be very motivated to do certain things that are of interest to them but resistive if it is not of interest to them. It may be that maintaining the focus of his attention is such a difficult task for him to do he is simply unable to do so unless he is highly motivated or over-focused. For a child like this, the statement "He can do perfectly well if he wants to" should not be interpreted as a criticism. It is an accurate statement and instructs those of us who are working with such a child that we need to organize our requests and instruction in the context of things that he is highly motivated about.

Several examples: One child could not sit still for a reading lesson in English, but she would concentrate for long periods of time to teach herself Japanese so that she could read Manga comic books. One boy was able to do well in his grade four math when all of the problems were given to him in the context of calculating numbers of Pokémon characters. One boy was unable to concentrate on anything to do with history or socials but he memorized all of the sports statistics for his favorite players. One highly social young woman was unwilling to put any effort into reading and her spelling was quite disabled until she discovered Facebook. With her extreme interest and much feedback from others about her spelling, both her reading and spelling improved beyond anything that was ever expected of her when she was in school.

Study guide

If you have noticed that the person you are supporting is sometimes able to focus well, make a list of which tasks and areas of interest seem to exceptionally motivate him or her. Think about ways you might be able to use these themes in a more general manner.

a.) Does the person you are supporting show over-focus in one or two specific areas? List these.
Have you observed if the person you are supporting is able to focus well, but only for a specific period of time (such as ten minutes then they become agitated)?

b.) Is there a predictable length of time the person you are supporting can concentrate before they burn out or shut down? How long is this?

Experiment and see if you can have a more peaceful day if you ask her to focus for only as long as it is easy and comfortable for her.

c.) Experiment: You will find that each child responds to their own unique style for gaining their attention. The goal is to find any unique circumstance where the child demonstrates that they <u>are</u> able to attend and are best able to respond without resistance or opposition.

i. Notice if the person you are supporting responds best to a lower or even whispered voice.

ii. Notice if the person you are supporting responds best when you get right in front of her and look her in the eyes.

iii. Notice if it helps if you first take both his hands and call his name.

iv. If you find some approach that seems to work for the person you are supporting make sure to communicate this within a behavior or teaching plan so that this becomes part of the person's "folklore" about how to avoid difficulties and challenging behavior.

If the person shuts down after 15 minutes, see what happens if you only ask for 10 minutes. Then give her a movement break or a quiet time break before expecting any more focused effort.

It is always helpful to make accommodations to a person who is easily distracted or inattentive. There are many things you can do that may help when you are uncertain about what may be the best thing to do.

- Gain eye contact before speaking.
- Keep your own language short (4-5 words)
- Speak, and then pause for several seconds. Then repeat what you have just said.
- Then have them repeat what you said.
- Visually demonstrate what you mean for the person to do. Use the objects you are describing in the manner that you wish the person to use the same objects.

Memory and complexity

Memory and complexity: *"I can only do or think about one thing at a time:"*

We have probably all worked with someone who could do well but only when given familiar things to do, one at a time. Often it turns out that it was the <u>complexity</u> that defeated the person's ability. For example: One adolescent youth had a good memory for what was said to him. He could do each part of a kitchen clean-up task when it was given to him one step at a time. Yet his ability to concentrate and do this work completely deteriorated if he was asked to do two or three things in a sequence and left on his own without further guidance.

Another youth was unable to concentrate at all when he was given ten math questions on a page. The same youth could concentrate well and was motivated when he was given only one math question on a page to do. (In his case he had a physical problem with visual scanning. Too many things on the page overwhelmed his visual processing ability. In another similar case it was that the child was emotionally overwhelmed by thinking "I'll never be able to do all of this work." In yet another similar case it was that the child was distracted and kept forgetting which problem he was working on so he did part of several different problems and completed none of them.)

a.) Think about these examples. Does any of this sound like it could possibly relate to the person you are supporting? Write down an example or two where you think complexity might be an issue?

b.) Experiment: See what happens if you give just one thing at a time to the person you are supporting. If you find a difference be sure that this becomes a part of the "folklore" included in the behavior or educational plan for the child.

Memory and complexity: *Too much information at once:*

When a person has a good attention span but is only "partially processing" what has been said to her this can look exactly like an attention deficit. Pay careful attention to whether she is missing parts of what you said (only getting the first part or the last part.) This could be due to problems with short term memory. If she does perfectly well when you only give her <u>one thing at a time</u> you can avoid the resistive behavior that may be due to her confusion and frustration that occurs when she is "corrected" for only doing part of what was asked of her.

A youth with an "invisible" memory problem will always confuse us when he can spontaneously speak in long paragraphs about interesting things he has done. He may be able to describe in great detail some movie or a videogame or a sporting event. Yet when we directly ask him to <u>repeat</u> what we have just said he might only repeat a few words. Most people <u>understand more</u> than they can say. It is hard to believe that some people can <u>say more</u> than they can understand.

Similarly, some youth are able to do complex actions that are very familiar to them. They can do well the things they have rehearsed for a long period of time such as a complex dance step or the words to a song they have repeatedly sung. The information has gotten into their long-term memory through blunt-force rehearsal. Yet, when you give them something unfamiliar to do they may be unable to copy more than one or two steps before they become completely lost, frustrated and reactive. These youth can be "smarter over time than in the immediate moment." Their long-term memory may be relatively intact, yet their short-term memory seems to only take in a small amount at a time.

Such a youth requires much more time to sit back and observe others. It can sometimes be helpful to let them wait until they ask to participate before placing any expectation on them to perform. Often these youth are quite competent and "perfectionist" and will not tolerate any attempt to get them to do something before they are ready to do it "on their own terms." Often these youth receive the label, "stubborn" or "always wants it to be his own way" when what is really happening is that they are trying <u>too hard</u> to be perfect. They may not be stubborn at all except about wanting to do what is being asked of them in the right way! They may only be stubborn about wanting to avoid failure.

Unless positive feedback is made explicit, the child may be unable to tell if they are doing the right thing or not. This makes it hard to learn from what would otherwise have been a positive experience. It is helpful to give enhanced feedback to the person with short-term memory difficulties while they are on track and doing well.

Complexity and conditional words: *"I just don't get it."*

Be aware of how you give information. Some people with challenging behavior and variable responses have great difficulty with the meaning of the small connecting words we use in ordinary language.

For example: A young man with good memory and good expressive language was unable to follow a simple direction to "pick up this or that." He could not do this until I explained to him that "or" meant "pick only one." Until his support staff observed this through a two-way mirror they could not accept or believe that such an otherwise smart person could have such a severe and "invisible" deficiency in his understanding. This helped to explain why he was so angry at people who said to him, "You are not listening to me!"

Other individuals may have great difficulty understanding the meaning of prepositional, positional, and relationship words such as "beside," "between," "behind," and "beyond." Interpreting such words requires a level of abstract thinking that for some people is just too difficult.

For example: I assessed one adult who tended to

go into a rage when something did not take place when she felt she had been "promised" that it would occur. She had good memory and could both read and repeat back long sentences from memory. Yet, she could not correctly respond to a simple command, "If there is a red one, pick up a black one." When I asked her, "Is there a red one?" she answered, "No." Then I repeated the question and she still picked up the black one. It turned out that she had never understood the simple explanations she was given "If it doesn't rain we will go bowling." She only processed "we will go bowling" and felt that she had been lied to when it rained and they did not go bowling.

A speech and language assessment will pick up on problems with conditional words. One way to avoid these problems is to try to phrase things "in the here and now."

Beware the use of time related words:

Time concepts are abstract. You will know if the child or youth has difficulty with time concepts when they are frequently and anxiously asking "How much longer?" You will know the person has difficulty with time concepts when they sit for an hour following the afternoon snack with their coat on and their backpack in their hands. They do understand that the bus comes after the afternoon snack, but they have no concept of "how long" it is when someone uses a conditional phrase and says to them, "not for another hour."

Persons who have a hard time with time concepts may not understand the meaning of the commonly used words such as "when," "not until," before," "after," "it's too early to go," and "don't be late." These same persons may do perfectly well if given a count-down timer and they are told, "do it till the bell rings!" That approach turns the "abstract" words about how long they should work into a "concrete" exercise.

There are some unique examples of people for whom time is JUST A NUMBER, not a concept! Unless you are familiar with just how handicapping lack of "time concepts" can be it is almost impossible to believe.

Examples showing TIME IS JUST A NUMBER for some people who were diagnosed with fetal alcohol spectrum disorder:

For one youth 11:50 did not mean 10 minutes before 12. If you told him it was time to get ready to leave for a 12 o'clock appointment, he would argue, "It's not 12 o'clock yet." He did not comprehend that it would take "ten minutes" to get from home to the place of appointment.

One man could be somewhere at 3:00, but could not "be back in 15 minutes." He was responsive and accurate when he was given a watch with a count-down timer and told to "come back when the buzzer goes off." (The exception was if he was distracted by someone who asked him to come with them. For this man, the most recent direction he was given "took over.")

Examples showing TIME IS JUST A NUMBER for some people who were diagnosed with autistic spectrum disorder:

At two o'clock, one child wanted to turn back the clock in his classroom to 12:00 which was before he had a melt-down. He said that he wanted to start the afternoon all over again and wipe out his mistake.

One youth in 2004 wanted to change all the calendars to 1998. He explained that 1998 had been a good year for him in school. Similarly, one 18 year old didn't understand why he couldn't go back to school at his elementary school where he had fewer problems.

One youth wanted to go back to where he was living so that he could finish a card game that was left unfinished when he moved out over five years previously.

One man was seen to be at the door of an office for an appointment at 10:00. He was seen to look at his watch and then walk away in frustration. We caught up to him and asked him where he was going and he said, "I missed my appointment, it is 10:01."

For people who have difficulty with time references in language there are often issues of resistive and oppositional behavior when it is time to transition from one activity to the next. They tend to not interpret the "warning cues" that are easy for other students to understand. If a child does not understand "warnings" about what is coming up next it is not helpful to give them consequences for not stopping doing what they think they are still supposed to be doing.

Teaching tips for people who have "trouble with time."

- To avoid unnecessary conflicts around transitioning between activities due to difficulty with time references and the use of conditional language it is almost always helpful to assist these individuals to make transitions with the explicit cue language, "All done XXX. Next, YYY."
- It is almost always useful to use explicit, positive language such as "we are doing <u>YYY</u> now!" while at the same time giving visual cues and physical guidance as necessary to assist the transition.

"Abstract" language about time may often lead to unnecessary melt-downs, confusion and frustration for a child and for those who are attempting to support her. Here are a number of examples about how to turn "abstract" time concepts into "concrete" information.

- Don't say "wait", say, "When the clock shows 10:15."
- Don't say "later", say, "Meet me at 3:07."
- Don't say "stop soon", say, "Watch or play till the timer goes off at 4:50. Then bring me the timer!"
- Don't say "hurry", say, "Where are my keys? Please bring them to me now. Go open the door to the car for me."
- Don't say "we'll be late", say, "We want to be on time at 12:30 for lunch!"

Study guide

Note the example of the smart mother of one anxious child who found that it was necessary to avoid all use of words relating to "past," "present," or "future." She found that she could avoid provoking an anxious response in her child. For the word "past," she said "used to be." For the word "present" she said "still is." For anything to do with the "future" she said, "We will have to check this out."

a.) Consider the person you are supporting and

how they relate to time words. Write down any examples you can think of where this might have been an issue.

b.) Have someone else observe and record how many times you use a conditional word such as "if", "or", "not until," "before" and "after."

c.) Discuss how you may rephrase your own comments so that you are speaking to the individual in the "here and now."

d.) As always, if there are certain words or phrases that make it easier for the individual you are supporting to remain in a peaceful relationship, be sure to add this to the "folk-lore" about the person in their behavior or teaching plan.

END

NOTE: Look for the next small books in this series. To be notified directly when these become available email to *challengingbehavior@shaw.ca*

WHO HAS TO CHANGE? TRYING THEIR HARDEST, DOING THEIR BEST!

The information in this article applies to any individual with a developmental disability who is dependent on others in some specific areas, and who does not learn from correction, or who does not 'get' why people are distressed with their behavior. While reading this think of children affected by autism spectrum disorder or fetal alcohol spectrum disorder. This same information applies equally well to youths and adults.

The effect on the child of impairment in brain functions during their developmental period.

Parents, teachers and support persons of individuals with some impairment in brain function that occurred during the child's developmental period such as autism spectrum disorder (ASD) or fetal alcohol spectrum disorder (FASD) are sometimes faced with episodes of extreme behavior. The first instinct we all follow is to use the same 'common sense' methods for controlling disruptive behavior that we would for any child.

In many ways impairment in brain function during the developmental period results in a person who thinks and learns in a different manner than a "normal' child. Aspects of the brain that are affected by impairments are rarely obvious until a child is old enough to interact with others in some inappropriate manner that does not seem to match the developmental progress of others. At first we tend to think this is due to immature behavior that the child will grow out of as they grow older and learn what is expected.

We may not recognize until a child is six or seven and finally begins school that there is "something else going on here." By this time, a child has already experienced several years of perceiving the world around him or her in a "different" manner that is unique to him or her self. By this time a child has already learned coping strategies that work for her, but which may be quite maladaptive for those who are trying to provide her with support. When these children act out in some excessive or violent manner those of us who support them need to ask ourselves several questions.

Whose problem is this? Who has to accommodate? Who has to learn something new to be able to solve these problems?

Learning cultural expectations:

When we are raising our children, our role as parents is to teach our children how to conform and to share in our cultural expectations for their behavior.

Things like "Do unto others as you would have them do unto you", "Don't interrupt while someone is speaking", or "It's polite to share..." we are all familiar with these statements. These are the type of slogans on the poster about "Everything I need to know in life I learned in kindergarten."

Every child is expected to accommodate and to

learn. We set the standards. We model correct social behavior. We remind and caution our children about the "rules".

We may try to make it fun to follow the social rules of our culture by offering positive consequences (rewards) for cooperation ("Whoever can use the quietest voice gets an extra book", "Whoever is the most polite gets to go on the computer first, etc.") When a child does not accommodate to our social expectations we may exercise direct control over the child by removing them from social opportunities. If they are just too tired to get along we may put them down for a nap or have them sit out a turn till they are calmed down and ready to cooperate. Often this is all that is required. These are the methods that we use to elicit voluntary cooperation and to socialize our children to grow up to become responsible, caring adults.

Some children still don't get our polite messages that their world insists that certain expectations be followed and that people around them have their own personal boundaries that they may not cross without consequences. We may use negative consequences (punishments) to teach them that the child does not have the right to always have their own way, or to bully others. We may use consequences such as sending them to their room. We may briefly take away privileges (later bed time, amount of television), or we may even "ground" the child from certain favoured activities. When we feel these methods are required for us to be able to maintain order and control, these are ways we educate our kids that their freedoms are related to their ability to accept some level of personal responsibility and to exercise self-control. Until the child shows a level of responsibility someone else will maintain control over the privileges that may take place in their world.

In Western culture, using these methods, children learn that there are boundaries. We eventually teach children that they are expected to act in a socially responsible manner, be accountable and responsible for their actions, and that they must accommodate some of their own behavior to be able to fit into the social norm.

And this works just fine for the greatest majority of our children. If we did not follow these cultural traditions our children would grow up "spoiled", expecting everything to be their way, whenever they want, and not become caring about the rights of others.

What is different about these children?

Here is the dilemma. For a very young child as well as with a child with some impairment in brain function that occurred during the child's developmental period, their mind may not perceive another persons' point of view. We understand that the only point of view of a very young child is their own, immediate perspective. They don't know what to do to "correct" their own behavior until an understanding support person reminds them that now is the moment when they have to remember to apply a social rule. ("What do you do with your hands?" "Use your soft voice"). Criticizing or challenging very young children does not assist their learning, is counter-productive and almost always makes things worse. The same is unfortunately true for older children who we have expected to "grow up" and who we think, "You should have learned by now" what is expected and to use self-control without constant reminders.

For a child who just doesn't "get" social expectations for self-control, he or she can sometimes see the meaning of what is being expected through a social story. Through social stories we gain the child's attention and we bring critical information to them, in story form, so that this can become their own point of view. These children may process, as through blinders, only what is concrete, and immediately apparent, in the immediate moment.

Some children with autism (ASD) or fetal alcohol (FASD) are not able to learn from negative consequences for their actions or correction following their mistakes. The child may be unable to learn from "losing" privileges because they don't make the connection between the loss of privilege and their own actions.

> NOTE: To deal with the "political realities" of operating within a school environment sometimes it may be necessary for other students and/or other teachers to observe the child receiving a "consequence." But the purpose of such a consequence would not be expected to cause the child to alter their behavior or to "learn from the experience."

However, a child who is unable to learn from "losing" may be quite capable of learning from "winning."

One child may not have a long enough attention span to connect what they did just before, with the consequence or correction that followed. However, if the same child is reminded about what is expected just ahead of time he or she may remember exactly what to do and may demonstrate self-control. But if the same child is brought into a problematic situation without <u>each time</u> re-educating him or her about the expectation, he or she may be unaware of what is expected and unable to self-monitor their own behavior. For these children it is necessary to focus them on what they need to do to be able to 'win'. Rather than focusing on what the child is doing 'wrong,' efforts need to be focused on rewarding the child for responding to your coaching and reminders to do appropriate, alternative action.

For some children, no matter how many times they have been through it before, for them each time they have an experience is like the very first time. If the child becomes frustrated or confused he or she may become very anxious. Such a child may <u>always</u> have to be coached and reminded.

The impact of anxiety on behavior:

Such children tend to not generalize a "lesson" learned from past experience to a new situation. If you admonish them about their behavior they may not know what to do to <u>self-correct</u> because they can't make the connection between previous and present situations. If this is the case, when you use the words, "no", "don't" and "stop" the child might only be "hearing" and feeling: "You don't like me", or "I'm bad". You may hear the child repeating to himself, 'I'm bad.'

Children growing up with these types of differences in their thinking and learning processes often become very emotionally fragile. They don't 'get' why people are so often distressed with their behavior. When the child experiences that others are distressed with them they may simply mirror or reflect back the very emotion of distress that is being shown towards them.

FOR THESE CHILDREN, IT IS VERY IMPORTANT TO REALLY LIKE THEM WHEN YOU ARE SPEAKING TO THEM. THEY SEEM TO WORK MORE OFF THE EMOTIONS OF THOSE AROUND THEM THAN THE WORDS AND ACTIONS OF THOSE WHO ARE GUIDING THEM. BEING EMOTIONALLY ANGRY TOWARDS SUCH A CHILD ALMOST ALWAYS FURTHER ESCALATES THEIR BEHAVIOR.

Most such children "telegraph" their anxiety by first becoming slightly agitated. Such behavior must be interpreted as communicative by their parents, teachers and other support persons. The message is 'come rescue me before I go out of control'. If the early signs of anxiety are not responded to the child may escalate to a point of self-injury or aggression until someone else intervenes to assist her to calm down.

Who has to change?

So here is the crux. Imagine an individual with ASD or FASD who, each time you organize the situation and remind them of expectations, he or she can do exactly what you expect, perfectly well. Yet each time you fail to put this much effort into anticipating what could possibly go wrong or fail to remedy every possible obstacle to success <u>ahead of time,</u> he or she becomes agitated, aggressive, self-injurious, withdrawn, and etc.

With such a child, the use of negative consequences only makes the child more reactive. Even when you use primarily positive consequences, the child may still remain dependent on you to structure and remind them about what to do. Such a child may never become totally independently able to be responsible for his own actions.

So back to the original question: Who has to change? Whose problem is this? Who has to accommodate? Who has to learn something new to be able to solve these problems?

The children being described here are not children that are "spoiled" by the parent or support person who is accommodating to his or her special needs. Some who are living with impairment in their brain function occurring during their developmental period may continually require the presence of someone else to keep his world orderly and structured. At the very least, he may predictably require at certain crucial moments the presence or immediate availability of someone else to keep his world orderly and structured.

Realistic and achievable expectations:

Such a child may not be able to achieve our cultural expectation for eventual independent functioning. But when someone is present to assist him to navigate through his life, the child may clearly show that he is willing and able to follow expectations and demonstrate adequate self-control.

Most of these reactive kids are very emotionally fragile. When they have a smile on their face they can be happy, cooperate, focus and work within their familiar repertoire. When they are distressed, confused, frustrated or anxious they tend to lose their ability to function and become very reactive. They may stop acting consciously, and drop down into a sensory-emotional state of generalized arousal. This can be devastating.

Caution about interference from others who just don't understand:

Another big dilemma is "outsiders" who don't see how much effort it takes to keep these kids "glued together" so that they can function at all. "Outsiders" see the accommodations made to protect these kids from "suffering consequences" of their actions. It is simply a fact that for some kids, they are only able to learn from positive rehearsal and do not seem to be able learn from their mistakes or from correction. For these kids accommodation must be made to protect them from negative consequences which lead to self-injurious and anxious, regressed behavior.

"Outsiders" may unknowingly blame support persons for "spoiling" the child. The "outsider" may not understand that the reason for giving additional positive feedback and rewards is to keep the child "glued together." The "outsiders" may give generalized "advice" that "the child has to learn", and "the world isn't always going to protect them." Or, '"No one is going to do that for them when they get to high school." But, for children who are capable when they are properly supported, yet unable to learn from negative experience, the world may have to <u>always</u> offer them a degree of additional feedback and protection.

These are not bad children and their parents are not bad parents. Often, they are both working heroically to overcome their developmental disabilities, intellectual handicaps and learning disabilities and to participate in the world wherever they are able.

NOTE: Look for the next small book in this series. To be notified directly when these are available email to *challengingbehavior@ shaw.ca*

CPSIA information can be obtained
at www.ICGtesting.com
Printed in the USA
LVIC06n1535110914
403630LV00024B/147

*9 7 8 1 4 9 5 9 6 9 3 3 1 *